R. VAUGHAN WILLIAMS

HODIE
(THIS DAY)

A CHRISTMAS CANTATA

For Soprano (C♯ - A′), Tenor (D♭ - A♭′),
and Baritone (D♭ - F or F♯) Soli,
Chorus and Orchestra

Pianoforte arrangement by Roy Douglas

OXFORD UNIVERSITY PRESS
MUSIC DEPARTMENT · 37 DOVER STREET · LONDON · W1X 4AH

NOTES

First performance: Three Choirs Festival, Worcester, 8th September 1954.

The cover picture of The Nativity, by Piero della Francesca, is reproduced here by courtesy of the Trustees of the National Gallery, London.

Full scores and sets of orchestral parts are available on hire, and a chorus edition is published.

The work is recorded on E.M.I. SCX 3570 (stereo), 33SX 1782 (mono).

Duration : approximately 50 minutes.

Orchestration

Flute I	Trumpets I and II
(Flute II)	(Trumpet III)
Flute III and Piccolo	Trombones I, II and III
Oboe I	Tuba
(Oboe II)	Timpani
Cor Anglais	Percussion
Clarinets I and II	Celesta
Bassoons I and II	(Harp)
(Double Bassoon)	Pianoforte
Horns I and II	(Organ)
(Horns III and IV)	Strings

Instruments in ( ) are cued and may be omitted.

HODIE
(THIS DAY)

A Cantata for Christmas

Nowell ! Nowell ! Nowell !
Hodie Christus natus est : hodie salvator apparuit :
Hodie in terra canunt angeli, laetantur archangeli :
Hodie exultant justi, dicentes : gloria in excelsis Deo : Alleluia.

From the Vespers for Christmas Day.

English Version.

Nowell ! Nowell ! Nowell !
Christmas Day, Christ was born on Christmas Day.
Christmas Day, Our Saviour was born on Christmas Day.
Christmas Day, on earth are angels singing, archangels
rejoicing. Christmas Day, rejoice ye just men, saying,
Glory to God in the highest : Alleluia.

Now the birth of Jesus Christ was on this wise : whenas his mother Mary was
espoused to Joseph, before they came together, she was found with child of
the Holy Ghost.

Then Joseph her husband, being a just man, was minded to put her away
privily. But while he thought on these things, behold, the angel of the Lord
appeared unto him in a dream.

ANGEL.

" Joseph, thou son of David, fear not to take unto thee Mary thy wife : for
that which is conceived in her is of the Holy Ghost. And she shall bring
forth a son, and thou shalt call his name Jesus :
He shall be great, and shall be called the son of the Highest : Emmanuel,
God with us."

From Matt. i. 18-21 and Luke i. 32

It was the winter wild,
While the Heaven-born child,
All meanly wrapt, in the rude manger lies ;
Nature in awe to him
Had doff'd her gaudy trim,
With her great Master so to sympathize.
. . . .
And waving wide her myrtle wand,
She strikes a universal peace through sea and land.

No war, or battle's sound,
Was heard the world around :
The idle spear and shield were high uphung ;
The hooked chariot stood
Unstain'd with hostile blood ;
The trumpet spake not to the armed throng ;
And kings sate still with aweful eye,
As if they surely knew their sovran Lord was by.

But peaceful was the night,
Wherein the Prince of light
His reign of peace upon the earth began :
The winds, with wonder whist,
Smoothly the waters kiss'd
Whispering new joys to the mild ocean,
Who now hath quite forgot to rave,
While birds of calm sit brooding on the charmed wave.

From Hymn on the Morning of Christ's Nativity. Milton.

IV. NARRATION. 28

And it came to pass in those days, that there went out a decree from Caesar
Augustus, that all the world should be taxed.   And all went to be taxed,
everyone into his own city.   And Joseph also went up unto the city of David,
which is called Bethlehem ; to be taxed with Mary his espoused wife, being
great with child.

And so it was that while they were there, the days were accomplished that
she should be delivered.   And she brought forth her first born son, and
wrapped him in swaddling clothes, and laid him in a manger ; because there
was no room for them in the inn.

From Luke ii. 1-7.

V. CHORAL. 30

The blessed son of God only
In a crib full poor did lie ;
With our poor flesh and our poor blood
Was clothed that everlasting good.
Kyrieleison.

The Lord Christ Jesu, God's son dear,
Was a guest and a stranger here ;
Us for to bring from misery,
That we might live eternally.
Kyrieleison.

All this did he for us freely,
For to declare his great mercy ;
All Christendom be merry therefore,
And give him thanks for evermore.
Kyrieleison.

Miles Coverdale, after Martin Luther.

VI. Narration.   35

And there were in the same country shepherds abiding in the field, keeping watch over their flock by night. And, lo, the angel of the Lord came upon them, and the glory of the Lord shone round about them : and they were sore afraid. And the angel said unto them,

" Fear not : for, behold, I bring you good tidings of great joy, which shall be to all people. For unto you is born this day in the city of David a saviour, which is Christ the Lord. And this shall be a sign unto you ; ye shall find the babe wrapped in swaddling clothes, lying in a manger."

And suddenly there was with the angel a multitude of the heavenly host praising God, and saying,

" Glory to God in the highest, and on earth peace, good will toward men. We praise thee, we bless thee, we worship thee, we glorify thee, we give thanks to thee for thy great glory ; O Lord God, heavenly King, God the Father Almighty."

" Let us now go even unto Bethlehem, and see this thing which is come to pass, which the Lord hath made known unto us."

And the shepherds came with haste, and found Mary, and Joseph, and the babe lying in a manger. And when they had seen it, they made known abroad the saying which was told them concerning this child. And all they that heard it wondered at those things which were told them by the shepherds.

Adapted from Luke ii. 8-17 *and the Book of Common Prayer.*

VII. The Oxen.   47

Christmas Eve, and twelve of the clock.
" Now they are all on their knees,"
An elder said as we sat in a flock
By the embers in hearth side ease.

We pictured the meek mild creatures where
They dwelt in their strawy pen,
Nor did it occur to one of us there
To doubt they were kneeling then.

So fair a fancy few would weave
In these years ! yet, I feel
If someone said on Christmas Eve,
" Come ; see the oxen kneel,

In the lonely barton by yonder coomb
Our childhood used to know,"
I should go with him in the gloom,
Hoping it might be so.

Thomas Hardy.

(*By permission of the Society of Authors, the Thomas Hardy estate, and the Macmillan Co. Inc., New York.*)

VIII. Narration.   50

And the shepherds returned, glorifying and praising God for all the things that they had heard and seen, as it was told unto them.

Luke ii. 20.

O well-spring of this All !
Thy father's image vive ;
Word, that from naught did call
What is, doth reason, live ;
The soul's eternal food,
Earth's joy, delight of heaven ;
All truth, love, beauty, good :
To thee, to thee be praises ever given !

O glory of the heaven !
O sole delight of earth !
To thee all power be given,
God's uncreated birth !
Of mankind lover true,
Indearer of his wrong,
Who dost the world renew,
Still be thou our salvation and our song !

William Drummond.

XIII. NARRATION. 67

Now when Jesus was born, behold, there came wise men from the east saying
" Where is he that is born King ? for we have seen his star in the east, and
are come to worship him."   And they said unto them, " In Bethlehem."
When they had heard that they departed ; and, lo! the star, which they saw
in the east, went before them, till it came and stood over where the young
child was.   When they saw the star, they rejoiced with exceeding great joy.
And when they were come into the house, they saw the young child with
Mary his mother, and fell down and worshipped him ; and when they had
opened their treasures, they presented unto him gifts ; gold, and frankincense,
and myrrh.

Adapted from Matthew ii. 1, 2, and 11.

XIV. THE MARCH OF THE THREE KINGS. 71

From kingdoms of wisdom secret and far
come Caspar, Melchior, Balthasar ;
they ride through time, they ride through night
led by the star's foretelling light.

Crowning the skies
the star of morning, star of dayspring calls,
lighting the stable and the broken walls
where the prince lies.

Gold from the veins of earth he brings,
red gold to crown the King of Kings.
Power and glory here behold
shut in a talisman of gold.

Frankincense from those dark hands
was gathered in eastern, sunrise lands,
incense to burn both night and day
to bear the prayers a priest will say.

Myrrh is a bitter gift for the dead.
Birth but begins the path you tread ;
your way is short, your days foretold
by myrrh and frankincense and gold.

Return to kingdoms secret and far,
Caspar, Melchior, Balthasar,
ride through the desert, retrace the night
leaving the star's imperial light.

Crowning the skies
the star of morning, star of dayspring, calls :
clear on the hilltop its sharp radiance falls
lighting the stable and the broken walls
where the prince lies.

Ursula Vaughan Williams. (by permission)

XV. CHORAL.   86

No sad thought his soul affright ;
Sleep it is that maketh night ;
Let no murmur nor rude wind
To his slumbers prove unkind ;
But a quire of angels make
His dreams of heaven, and let him wake
To as many joys as can
In this world befall a man.

Promise fills the sky with light,
Stars and angels dance in flight ;
Joy of heaven shall now unbind
Chains of evil from mankind,
Love and joy their power shall break,
And for a new born prince's sake ;
Never since the world began
Such a light such dark did span.

Verse 1. Anon.
Verse 2. Ursula Vaughan Williams. (by permission)

(ix)

In the beginning was the Word, and the Word was with God, and the Word was God. In Him was life; and the life was the light of men. And the Word was made flesh, and dwelt among us, full of grace and truth. Emmanuel, God with us.

Adapted from John i. 1-14.

Ring out, ye crystal spheres,
Once bless our human ears,
If ye have power to touch our senses so ;
And let your silver chime
Move in melodious time,
And let the bass of heaven's deep organ blow ;
And, with your ninefold harmony,
Make up full consort to the angelic symphony.

Such music (as 'tis said),
Before was never made,
But when of old the sons of morning sung,
While the Creator great
His constellations set,
And the well-balanced world on hinges hung ;
And cast the dark foundations deep,
And bid the weltering waves their oozy channel keep.

Yea, truth and justice then
Will down return to men,
Orbed in a rainbow ; and, like glories wearing,
Mercy will sit between,
Throned in celestial sheen,
With radiant feet the tissued clouds down-steering ;
And heaven, as at some festival,
Will open wide the gates of her high palace hall.

From Hymn on the Morning of Christ's Nativity. Milton.

HODIE
(THIS DAY)
A Christmas Cantata
for Soprano, Tenor, and Baritone Soli,
Chorus, and Orchestra

Pianoforte arrangement by
Roy Douglas

R. VAUGHAN WILLIAMS

I. PROLOGUE
[CHORUS STANDS]

★ The tenors may be reinforced by high baritones (compass up to F sharp);
when the tenor parts divide the baritones should, of course, sing the lower part.

★The English words may be sung at the discretion of the conductor, but the composer would much prefer the Latin.

4

This Day

6

This Day

10

This Day

12

14

This Day

16

This Day

This Day

II NARRATION

[TREBLES STAND : CHORUS REMAINS STANDING]

20

narration
Angel & Truth

This Day

This Day

III SONG

[S. & A. REMAIN STANDING : T. & B. SIT]

24

This Day

This Day

IV NARRATION

[T. & B. STAND : S. & A. REMAIN STANDING]

To be taxed with Ma - ry his es - pous - ed wife, be-ing great with child.

And so it was that while they were there, the days were ac - com -

- - plished that she should be de - liv - ered. And she brought forth her first born

son, and wrapped him in swad - dling clothes, and laid him in a man - ger;

be - cause there was no room for them in the inn.

Segue No. V

This Day

V CHORAL

[CHORUS REMAINS STANDING]

32

for us free-ly, For to de-clare his great mer-cy; All Christ-en-

for us free-ly, For to de-clare his great mer-cy; All Christ-en-

us free-ly, For to de-clare his great mer-cy; All Christ-en-

-dom be mer-ry there-fore, And give him thanks for ev-er-more,

-dom be mer-ry there-fore, And give him thanks for ev-er more,

-dom be mer-ry there-fore, And give him thanks for ev-er more,

VI NARRATION

[CHORUS REMAINS STANDING]

This Day

This Day

38

This Day

D

40

This Day

This Day

This Day

ly - ing in a man - ger._____ And

when they had seen it, they made known a - broad___ the say - ing which was told___

___ them con - cern - ing this child. **12** And all they__ that heard it won -dered at

those things which were told them by the shep – herds._____

This Day

VII SONG
The Oxen

CHORUS SITS
TREBLES SIT

sat in a flock___ By the emb-ers in hearth-side ease.___ We

pic-tured the meek, mild creat-ures where They dwelt in their straw-y pen,

Nor did it oc-cur to one of us there___ To doubt they were

Poco animato

kneel-ing then.___ So fair a fan-cy few would weave In

these years! Yet, I feel, If some-one said on Christ-mas Eve,___

VIII NARRATION

Attacca No. IX

This Day

IX PASTORAL

[TREBLES SIT]

The shep-herds sing;____ and shall I sil-ent be?____ My God, no hymn for thee?____ My soul's a shep-herd too:____ a flock it feeds____ Of thoughts and words and deeds.____ The pas-ture is thy word;____

*The 𝅘𝅥𝅭 of the 9/8 equals the 𝅘𝅥 of the 3/4 throughout this movement

54

Wait: Bass solo (IX)

X NARRATION

[TREBLES STAND]

But__ Ma-ry kept all these_ things,__

and pond-ered them__ in her heart.__

XI LULLABY

[CHORUS S. & A. STAND]

Sweet was the song the Vir-gin

This Day

58

This Day

60

This Day

XII HYMN

[CHORUS S. & A. SIT]
[TREBLES SIT]

This Day

Ten.

With di - a - man - - tine bars, Your ar-ras rich___ up -
(Ob. & Cor Ang. with voice)

p Strs. Clars. Fag.

pizz.

Ten.

- hold, Loose all your bolts and springs, Ope wide your leaves___ of_

(and Hns.)

(and Fls.)

Ten.

gold, That in your roofs___ may come the King___

fp

f

Tutti ff

Ten.

___ of_ Kings, the King_ of Kings.___

p

ff

This Day

63

This Day

64

This Day

This Day

XIII NARRATION

[TREBLES STAND]

heard that they de -part - ed;_____ and lo!_____ the star, which they saw in the East, went be -fore them_____ till it came and stood ov - er where the young child was._____ When they saw the star, they re - joiced_____ with ex - ceed - ing great__ joy.

This Day

And when they were come in-to the house, _____ they saw the young child _____ with Ma- ry his_ moth-er, and fell_ down and wor-shipped him: and_ when they had o-pened their_ treas-ures, they pre- -sent-ed un-to him gifts; _____ gold, _____ and frank-in-cense and myrrh. _____

XIV THE MARCH OF THE THREE KINGS

[CHORUS STAND]

F

This Day

From king-doms of wis-dom sec-ret and far

come Cas-par, Mel-chi-or, Bal-tha-sar; they

calls,_____ light - ing the sta - ble and the brok - en walls_____

where _____ the prince lies._____

This Day

80

This Day

82

This Day

This Day

84

This Day

Attacca
subito No. XV

Breathe in crescen only

small group
Emp: his
verse

XV CHORAL

[CHORUS REMAINS STANDING]

★Verse 1 to be sung by a Semi-chorus of from 8 to 16 voices (in this
verse boys' voices are not to be used); 2nd Verse to be sung full.

This Day

XVI EPILOGUE

[CHORUS REMAINS STANDING]

This Day

This Day

★Note : ♩ ♩ ♩ a shade slower than ♪♪♪ of No. III

This Day

This Day

92

This Day

This Day

This Day

This Day

9/26   Group
           Tour presentation

Dec 1 ± 2 (3 pm)   Nov 26 ± 28 = orchestra rehearsals
    (8 pm)

10/20   Men's Chorus w/ Boston Common